7PROSE

Franz Wright

7PROSE

Marick Press
Grosse Pointe Farms, Michigan

for Sandra Merrick

a
thought,
barefoot

—Sappho

CONTENTS

MANUSCRIPT SCORE OF MESSIAEN'S END OF TIME QUARTET

By the rivers of Babylon . . .

Where is your hand now, architect of the unseeable, syrinxes' harpist and departed sower of this rainbow made up of the voices of extinct birds perched as shivering notes along barbed wire. Do you remember that place, still endure it, like a slight limp, or a small undivulgable homesickness, are such things erlaubt where you are? That place where no one would dare weep, let alone sit down. Where the captors required of nobody a song, indifferently allowing yours; even listening politely with their sad attack-dogs' eyes awhile. Before shrugging, and getting back to work.

The Death of St. Teresa of Avila

When it had become clear that the deceased was not about to relinquish either the mysterious failure to rot or pervasive and oddly annoying fragrance of roses in which she'd been lying in bed for some months wearing an expression of profoundly childlike happiness, shining eyes wide open, a white sheet pulled up to her chin, the final reaction of her associates was unpleasant, to say the least. It was as if such an unprecedented period of mourning, awe, enforced silence and increasing bewilderment over how to proceed with the funeral had nourished and gradually allowed the dark gestation of a general but mutually unacknowledged wish until, in one sudden and uncontrollable venting of lust to acquire sacred relics, they simply tore the body apart. The ownership of its various limbs (and anatomically let's just leave it at that) was then savagely contested as if by black cassocked gorillas. One hastens to add that this deplorable but surely unpremeditated behavior was instigated by a single individual acting alone, none other than Teresa's longtime acquaintence and confidante Father Gracián who comported himself from the first in the most discreet manner, believing himself to be completely unobserved when he stole into the glowing silence of her room with the kitchen's meat cleaver concealed in his sleeve and a cutting board tucked deftly under his arm and, coughing loudly to cover the sound of the blow, hacked off one of her weightless white hands.

Cutting

All the Sylvia Plath fan clubs will be meeting on campus tonight, same as any other night, same as any other college, at undisclosed hours, girls alone in their dorm rooms busily calculating the number of carrot sticks they'll be allowed to consume the next day and scolding their teddy bears in funny voices, while they wait for it to be time to take powerful long-acting amphetamines, you know, their *meds,* legally provided by their psychiatrists for a slight fee covered by their parents, the ones that help them concentrate better on what they will soon be doing with their razors, oh see the children's brightly lit party boat traveling faster and faster through the darkness toward a gigantic waterfall of blood.

BEES OF ELEUSIS

*Unless a grain of wheat goes into the ground and dies, it remains nothing
but a grain of wheat . . .*
    John 12:24

The ingredients gathered, a few small red tufts of the dream spoor
per sheaf of Demeter's blonde wheat, reaped in mourning, in
silence, ground up with the pollen and mixed into white wine and
honey. These stored forms of light taken under the ground. Taken
by mouth. First those who by birth hold in secret the word; then
placed on the tongues of the new ones, into whose ears it is meant
to be whispered. Word murdered, forgotten so long ago, placed as
a kiss on the lips of the soon to be no longer breathing who mean
to enter death with open eyes, with mouths saying death, *what*
death? We have no word for it in our country where the bride of a
brighter oblivion reigns. Not the purple-haired god but the child
queen, the raped girl, come back from the dead hand in hand with
the child she conceived there, returned in a resurrected virginity,
wind through green wheat. Present-day site of a minor oil refinery
in Christ. Although by the tenth generation already the children of
light ("in their dark garments") had trampled and smashed and
generally force-fucked the two thousand years of this precinct and
its holy meal, intolerable mirror. Men who'd designed and bowed
down to a law derived from the sayings of one who appeared here
to say that the law is abolished, it is too late, all that is over with.
Men who bungled their way through the next eighteen centuries
before finally descending into the earth themselves, and what they
found there they used, and we thank you for destroying the destroy-
ers of the world. And here at the end this is as good as any other
entrance to the underplace, journey of the fallen leaf back to the
branch, to the bees of Eleusis among olive blossoms, untroubled
among crimson wildflowers. Four thousand years later: same
flowers, same bees.

Dim sun-checkered path through the forest, the perishing limbs loose their leaves; were they mine I would gladly let go all my gold leaves to carpet the ground her feet walk on, though she merely frown, forget I lived, and hurry on, for she must not be late; for reasons not at present time if ever known she can't be late. She hurries on. She only knows that they are waiting. They are waiting. They are longing for her at this very moment. All year long they have been pining for her, waiting and listening, listening through sleep for the steps they know, the little knock, the child she was they most intently listen for and wait. The child she never was but will be now, if somewhat tall, the instant the front door starts opening as though by itself and the option to enter is offered, apparently. They rejoice, at mere sound of her steps were already rejoicing, though no one will say so; no one knows how that is done, how to make the appropriate face even. They wish in their way to delight at the sight of her, even if it is all they can do to grunt something in greeting, so great is their happiness that she has come, is standing there in person. But for her they have little to live for. It's dying they live for in fact, and tv. Somebody hands the remote to her, this honor is done her, and gestures sit down. Want a coke, want a cookie, they mutter, it sounds like that, eyes still intent on the set with the sound off, familiar room otherwise dark, curtains drawn. There in its light they all sit: Father Blind, Mother Monster, now her, the faculty of speech regressed already to that of a nine-year-old irreparably shy with terror, sick with hope. She can't say she is comfortable yet with being seated in this vast armchair, her feet barely touching the floor; or with the prospect of having to sleep in a bed half her length, in her old room, or with lying there in utter darkness frozen, unable to move when they enter, tongue drawn back into her throat. But then she will be dreaming won't she? The visit itself may be some kind of dream, that is still vaguely possible, a hope entertained, resorted to when necessary, when painful and unheard-of things were occurring to her body, for example, no cessation of them yet in sight, in previous years, those unending years of actually living there, possessing in fact no memory whatsoever of ever having woken up anywhere else. For the time being though she is still sitting here, right next to Mother the fixed smiling glare and her husband the mumbled joke nobody gets, they appear to be sleeping, reclined in their chairs, all year long they've been sleeping, sleeping as snow fell, blowing all around the house, spring branches tapping at windows, each alone in their rooms, summer fields white for harvest, then leaves, golden leaves falling, leaves of my dying, dying to see his eyes, hear his voice saying my name, once again he has come here to save me, to buy me things, teach me how monsters have monsters, that's right, the tormented torment, the abandoned abandon, charismatically numb, cold, surviving, the last ones left standing, and how shall they warm someone else so very much themselves in need of one to come and save them from that arctic horror they have been crossing on foot all their lives, the last companion eaten, the graves of my footprints erased long ago, dying of loneliness there in my cubicle, waiting for someone to resuce me, someone to rescue, it comes to the same thing. *Save me . . . I miss you . . .* All the while they were sleeping, they slept as the seasons were changing around them, waiting for this day, Mother Beat You Daily Into Speechless Deafness, Father Blind To It All, *I'm sorry dear we just don't have the money for a hearing aid right now,* blue soundless tv, and look: there's Brother Rapist, unnoted, unmentioned, the originless weeping ignored, ignored knock at the back door, the knocking that goes on and on, forwarding address unknown; and Sister Silent is sitting here too in the bad light, the perpetually downcast gaze, the amputated tongue, forever nodding *yes yes yes* as she's mouthing the words of the miniature Bible she carries at all times, never getting beyond the first page, from under her pillow it slowly recites itself, such a kind voice saying everything's fine, everything is going to be all right abruptly followed by a stream of loudly whispered accusations, each one true! But he didn't really mean it, my peace, my beloved, while we're waiting for her to turn up, it seems like all we ever do, poor little elder sister still so far and maybe lost awhile but on the straight road once again, surely, and she shall wear gold, golden leaves to adorn her, to guide her here, nodding, now and then slapping herself in the face, hard, trying to shake off the dream she keeps falling into, earth opening under her, the dream of walking some-place else, anywhere, I must wake up now she's saying, yes, she is so close, I can already hear her, but here in Kindertotenwald the way is long, the roads unnamed, etiquette strange, changing from day to day, minute to minute, for example: is it correct to comment admiringly on a family friend's shiny new fang dentures? There I can't help you. The house must be close by now. So what does one say this time, what does one do, when the sardonic greetings cease? You're asking *me*? Cringing hugs, possibly. Shake a chill and weightless hand. Kiss a cheek smelling faintly of stale lilac and rotting meat. Take an axe to them all, shrieking, exalted, hunting them from room to room, screaming the scream that will never be over? Beats me. And how did they manage it do you imagine all those years keeping their true lives concealed from the neighbors and look at them now in their ultimate cunning somehow they have totally changed their appearance I mean past recognition you feel who are these shrunken frail elderly people who've taken the place of our parents and where did they bury them old people no one would ever suspect victims now think of that and abandoned nobody to care for them here in their long dusty nap with the grass growing up to the windows the household falling down around them all on account of this one thankless child Miss big city fake blonde and self-centered daughter. Who cannot be bothered. Yet here she is again. And why? Why? Why do we still go on phoning them visiting feted and fed by our torturers why did we not at eighteen leave and never look back and completely forget them, I know, the need from time to time the need to prove they're really there you can see them have proof that they actually lived are even living still at a listed address and not just in your head and besides. Where else did you ever fit in, tell the truth, and where else is a monster to turn, so close now, what else can you do turn around and go home, and what home would that be? Turn around and go back to that arduously perfected impersonation of one of the normal, fuck the normal, where were they when we needed them, and how could they know, how comprehend this poor sorrow, the guilt, the humiliating and undisobeyable hunger to *somewhere* belong, just to rest for a day, and be for once this crippled child and how much she has loved.

CAN YOU SAY THAT AGAIN

My stepfather was busy splitting my stepmother's skull with an axe, which struck me as excessive behavior even for him—oh, I see: she'd first flown in the window and folding her black vespertilian wings had bitten his neck pretty bad, which quite naturally resulted in instantaneous rabies, then their mutual demise, why didn't I think of that? A conical mountain rose in the distance, a road winding around and around it like the thread of a screw, on it children in white chadors descending slowly in song (the two of them reborn in their company), I never heard anything like it. Each, then, releasing from hands now unfolded from prayer scarlet moths who darkened the air, the sound of their voices like faraway choirs heard while dying by fire for the cause.

The Last

Now we will leave behind poetry and paranoia and get real for a while. This is now me speaking, it really is, at least insofar as I comprehend that word and keeping in mind that in my case a degree of relativity is bound to come attached to it, a range of entities.

Where to begin. At times when this so-called me is by himself and he is mad; all right, when *I* am by myself and very very angry, either at something or somebody else or, just as often, myself, I will suddenly hear said self snarling with a viciousness and conviction that astounds me, "Jesus Christ was a son of a bitch!"

I honestly can't help it: it leaps right out of my mouth before I have a chance to reconsider, or at least to bite down on and kill it, mouth filling with blood. And I ask you. Why in the world to someone unabashedly in love with that Person would such a shockingly cheap and ugly string of words ever occur, or be given, so that he must then contemplate them, appalled, for some time, these dull jewels of self-disgust? I try to imagine kind and considerate people I know saying something like that and feel coming over me, each time it happens, a cold blush of loathing and shame.

Well, if you'd like to know why, and even if you wouldn't, I will present my theory on the matter. Actually it can be summed up in the single word *Dad*.

It seems likely these words come so readily to me because they are the very ones (among others even more inventive) I spent my early childhood listening to the poor man mutter, scream, or utter—utter in the tone of voice in which somebody might threaten to kill you and mean it.

I have worked it out mathematically, rounding it off on the charitable side, and it seems that by the time I was seven years old I would have overheard that absurd imprecation employed approximately one thousand times. It made quite an impression.

As is widely known, my father had a way with words. And believe me, he said other things, too; things you do not want me to put in your mind.

I love my father more than any human being I have ever known.

Want to hear another one? Ok, same saintly lover of animals and other people's children.

He abruptly appeared once, emerging from his study with a belt in his hand, completely nude (this detail still mystifies me, but it does possess the rhetorical virtue of being virtually impossible to make up) and in an unspeaking, cold, methodical and *nude* rage he beat the black puppy he had just the other day given me for happily running in circles and barking while he was attempting to type. I was four. Perhaps my sole vivid memory of being four is looking on while he whipped it; and he whipped it until it vomited.

The only person I have ever known who makes credible Miguel de Unamuno's mysterious admonishment *live in a manner that would render your early death a disaster to the world* is my father.

One Saturday morning when I was somewhat older and my brother was still a toddler, he happened to be stumbling hysterically after my dad—or maybe it was my mother. Same difference.

(Remind me someday to tell you all about the monster who gave birth to me.) Whoever it was was no doubt obliviously absorbed in grave matters of intellect or art. Anyway, my brother had other things in mind, clearly requesting in his way some little moment of comfort affection or simple attention only to find one of his forefingers suddenly severed by the bathroom door slammed in his face. But it's all right, they sewed it back on somewhere, and my brother doesn't remember a thing. I can recall waiting alone— an activity at which I was, already, highly practiced—for my mother and brother to return in the car. You see, my father never learned to drive; and besides, he was extremely busy in his study during the time they were gone, this being I was seeking all my life with despair, finding him here and there for a time, so I thought, and pressing on. The being I sought, always failing, always rising and trying again, all my life to become.

So it has always been, and so it always will be—no, *not* always, not before I was, and for sure not soon. And so I go on working, my peace, sundial of my death. I go on working for the night is coming when no one may work. When no one has to anymore.

ACKNOWLEDGEMENTS

"The Death of St. Teresa of Avila" & "Cutting" first appeared
in *Salmagundi.*

"Can You Say That Again" was published as a broadside by Ray
Amarosi and Katie O'Donnell at North River Press, Massachusetts

I would like to thank Mariela Griffor, Rhonda May Karson, Peg
Boyers, Michael Dickman, Fady Joudah, David Young, Kristen
Smith, Michelle Olney, Deborah Garrison, Emma Bolden, Peter
Lograsso, Olga Broumas, Madeleine Barnes, Ana Bozicevic-
Bowling, Natalie Kusz, Valzhyna Mort and Elizabeth Oehlkers
Wright for their friendship, and for many inspired suggestions
and corrections.

F. W.

ISBN: 978-1934851-17-3

Cover art by Franz Wright

Printed in the United States

MARICK PRESS
P.O. Box 36253
Grosse Pointe Farms
Michigan 48236
www.marickpress.com

www.ingramcontent.com/pod-product-compliance
Lightning Source LLC
Chambersburg PA
CBHW022352040426
42449CB00006B/848